Forty Days of Financial Meditation

Dear Shuni,

    The Lord is pleased with you + He is going to start downloading strategies for success.

      Monique

FORTY DAYS OF FINANCIAL MEDITATION

Find Financial Freedom
Through God's Word

M. Olette Etheridge

Atlanta, Georgia

Forty Days of Financial Meditation
Find Financial Freedom Through God's Word
Copyright © 2013 M. Olette Etheridge

For further information, please contact
zoe2107@att.net

Layout & Design: Susan L.Volkert
Editing: Scott Roberts

Library of Congress Control Number:
2013919091
Printed in the United States of America
ISBN: 978-0-615-89334-1

Acknowledgements

First and foremost, I want to thank my Lord and Saviour Jesus Christ who has allowed me to write this book to encourage and to enlighten all who read it. I also want to thank all of my students who I have taught in the past various financial principles. My prayer for all of you is that you get and stay out of the bondage of debt. I also want to thank my parents who were my first teachers. They taught me basic principles such as make sure you bring in more money than you make and to always pay your bills on time. Finally, I want to thank my husband for always encouraging me to complete the book.

Contents

Introduction

Have you ever come to a major intersection in the middle of rush hour, and did not know which way to go? Or have you ever had a deep desire to pursue a dream, but did not know what to do first? Or have you started on a path in life where you reached a certain point, and felt stuck? Well *40 Days of Financial Meditation* is a book that will drop spiritual nuggets that will give you financial direction, jump start your finances, unravel the mystery of financial blockages, and speak life into your finances through the word of God. When the Lord formed, and breathed life into the nostrils of Adam, He also breathed His creative power into him. The fullness of God's spirit was now abiding in man. We have the ability to speak life or death over situations, circumstances, and things. Which one will you choose, life or death? I encourage you to choose life. *40 Days of Financial Meditation* will help you breathe life, bring revelation, and stir up your God given creative abilities regarding finances. God has given us his full authority here on earth through Jesus Christ. As his ambassadors we have the ability to command the atmosphere to change on our behalf according to his word. The Lord told Joshua to keep His word on his lips, meditate on it day and night, do everything that is written in it, then his way will be prosperous and successful. So as you mediate on the principles, and pray the prayers through faith know that the Lord hears you, and things are moving in your favor. So get ready to breathe life into the nostrils of your finances. As you breathe life over your finances, release your faith to receive life. Before the day of Pentecost Jesus breathed over the disciples and told them to receive the Holy Spirit. Every day you wake up God is breathing life over you. I pray that you receive life into your finances, apply the Godly principles in this book, and experience financial blessings.

Forty Days of Financial Meditation

DAY 1

Three Things Part 1:

Cravings

Have you ever wondered why you could not get ahead in your finances? You may be trapped by the lust of the flesh, the lust of the eye, or the pride of life. You can learn about these sins in 1 John 2:16. The New International Version Bible states, "For everything in the world – the cravings of sinful man, the lust of the eyes, and the boasting of what he has and does – comes not from the Father but from the world." One of these three things – or any combination of these three things, may prevent you from totally breaking through financially.

The craving of sinful man is really the lust of the flesh. Sexual immorality, overeating, and addiction to narcotics are all ways to lust after the flesh. All of these addictions keep us from breaking through financially. For instance, sexual immorality may lead to a costly divorce. If you are looking for instant gratification, dealing with unforgiveness, or just disobeying God's word, it may be because of this same lust. The lust of the flesh tells you to do what makes you feel good NOW – regardless of the consequences. Ask God why you do what you do.

God forgives us of all our sins, but we still have to endure the consequences of our decisions. The truth is that you really need a touch from the true and living God to get out of the trap. So did the Samaritan woman with five husbands who was at the well in John 4:7-10 (NIV). Jesus had asked her for a drink of water. She told Jesus that he had nothing to draw with and that the well was too deep. But, He did it anyway. Jesus is the true and living water.

Many of us are like that Samaritan woman, running from one relationship or bad habit to another. We are often so burdened with these temporary fixes that we do not recognize the Lord. The temporary fixes are causing us to dig a deeper hole financially and emotionally.

Ask God:

Please touch me and help me to recognize that I am
always in your presence and
held accountable for my decisions –
both financial and otherwise.

DAY 2

Three Things Part 2:

Lust of the Eyes

Can you say *shopaholic?*

Do you belong to the "I wanna" club? You know, constantly whining, "I want this and I want that."

Are you trying to keep up with the Joneses and impress people who don't really care about you anyway? Well, let me ask you a question about the Joneses: How much do you know about their finances? Do you have any idea what kind of debt they are burdened with? Do you know if they have any money saved for their children's college education? Don't envy anyone else's possessions. You don't know how they got them. It may be killing them to keep up appearances.

The lust of the eyes is one of the oldest sins in the Bible. Eve ate the fruit because she lusted with her eyes. Genesis 3:16 states "When the woman SAW that the fruit of the tree was good for food and PLEASING to the EYE ... she took some and ate it." People are still dealing with Eve's bad decision. How long are you going to allow material things to control you? Do you not realize that every decision that you make affects three to four generations after you? How will this affect your retirement account? Your emergency fund? It's important to think about the consequences of your decisions.

According to Lee Jenkins in *Taking Care of Business*, "Blacks on average are six times more likely than Whites to own a Mercedes, and the average income of a Black that buys a Jaguar is about one-third less than that of a White purchaser of the luxury vehicle." I believe that many of our people do not understand the opportunity-cost of their decisions. Opportunity-costs is defined as the opportunities forgone in the choice of one expenditure over others. The opportunity-cost of purchasing a Mercedes with a $900 monthly payment for the next five years at 8% interest is $66,129.17! These type of purchases into depreciating assets will keep this cultural group behind for generations to come.

Ask God:

***Please help me to exercise
some self-control and to see
beyond tomorrow.***

DAY 3

Three Things Part 3:
Pride of Life

Have you ever met people who constantly brag about their accomplishments, where they live, or how much money they make? Don't they just make you ill? There is nothing wrong with achieving your goals, but there is a problem when people have overinflated self-perceptions. People must realize that according to Deutoronomy 8:18 (NIV), "But remember the Lord your God, for it is He who gives you the ability to obtain wealth."

How about this: Have you ever met someone who had compulsive behavior – like an extreme shopping habit? Would that person get offended when you offered him or her financial advice? You should know that the spirit of offense is rooted in pride. Proverbs 11:2 (NIV) states, "When pride comes, then comes disgrace, but with humility comes wisdom."

What's wrong with pride? Pride keeps people from

humbling themselves before God and changing their ways. Pride prevents you from getting on the right track with God. Pride causes you to want to deny that you have a bad shopping habit which causes you to remain financially destitute. Pride refuses to acknowledge that what you have and do comes from the Lord. When you suffer from pride, you exalt yourself above God. According to Exodus 20:3 (NIV), God said, "You shall not have any gods before me." What are you making into your God?

Tell God:

I humble myself before you.

DAY 4

Do You Feel Stuck?

Have you ever wondered why you work so hard at your job and you're not getting anywhere?

Maybe you need to view where you are from another perspective. Is this job one of many streams of income? Does God have you on assignment to reach someone? Remember that the great commission to make disciples for Christ is not just for the preachers.

Consider what your short-term goals are (0 -1 year), what your mid-term goals are (5 to 10 years) and what your long-term goals are (more than 10 years). You have to know what you were created to do. Usually, you can figure that out by asking yourself what you would do if you were totally debt free? Ask yourself what natural gift or talent you have. If you start making plans to position yourself (i.e., get out of debt or save up seed money) to answer that calling, you can do what you want.

Finally, has God given you the vision of what you are supposed to do? Have you done what Habakkuk

2:2-3 (NIV) advises? Did you "write down the revelation and make it plain on tablets so that a herald may run with it. For the revelation awaits an appointed time; it speaks of the end and will not prove false. Though it linger, wait for it; it will certainly come and will not delay"?

God said:

Write it down, and speak to it.

DAY 5

Do You Love God?

Okay. Let's be honest. Many of the financial troubles we have suffered are due to pure disobedience to the Lord. It is not always because of environment or upbringing. You choose whether to be poverty-stricken or prosperous. John 14:15 (NIV) states, "If you love me, you will obey what I command." Does your lifestyle reflect your love for God? Have you conformed to the ways of this world, e.g., living with your boyfriend/girlfriend, not tithing, harboring unforgiveness? Remember, God is everywhere all of the time. God honors obedience. No matter what, you have to trust and obey Him. Deuteronomy 30:19 (NIV) states, "This day I call heaven and earth as witnesses against you that I have set before you life and death, blessings and curses. Now choose life, so that you and your children may live." Remember the choice is yours.

Tell yourself:

I will obey Him.

Day 6

Windows of Heaven

God promised in Malachi 3:10 (b) Amplified Version that He "will open the windows of heaven for you and pour out a blessing, that there shall not be room enough to receive it." The only way for you to open the floodgates of heaven is to be obedient in giving your tithe. When you do this, you are operating under His divine direction. You are operating in God's zone. You will have no doubt of what your vision, purpose, or direction is for your life. On the other hand, if you are not tithing, you are not operating under an open heaven. You will always struggle. You will never be content. Every time that you get money, something will happen to take that money from you. For instance, you may earn a bonus at work, and then lose it because your car breaks down.

Malachi 3:11 (NIV) tells us that – for those who are tithing – God will prevent pests from devouring their crops. Well, if you are not tithing, this does not apply to you. Your crops (i.e., money) will always be eaten up. According to Matthew 13:3,4 (NIV), "A farmer (God) went out to sow his seed. As he was scattering the seed, some fell along the path, and the birds ate it up." Later on in this chapter, Jesus states in verse 14 (NIV) that "you will be ever hearing but never understanding; you will be ever seeing but not perceiving." Those who do not heed to God's word will not inherit the Kingdom.

Action step:

Start tithing.

DAY 7

Preparation

Preparation is one of the main keys to financial success. You have written down your financial goals. Now do you know what it takes to achieve those goals? Do you need to stop eating out so much? Do you need to acquire some additional skills or go back to school? One of my favorite chapters in the Bible is Matthew 25. Matthew 25: 1-5 talks about the ten bridesmaids. Five were foolish, and five were wise. The foolish ones took their lamps but did not take any oil with them. (That is like driving on an empty tank for a long road trip.) The wise ones took their lamps and additional oil with them. When it was time to meet the groom, the foolish ones had to go out at midnight and buy some oil. (I wonder who was open at midnight back in the Bible days? They must have purchased their oil at a premium!) The wise bridesmaids did not give them any of their oil. I wonder what the foolish bridesmaids were doing while the wise bridesmaids were purchasing their additional oil in advance. Were they sleeping, watching TV, vacationing, or procrastinating? How many times have you missed opportunities because you have not prepared yourself? So, what are you waiting for? Start preparing now.

Action step:

Stop procrastinating.
Take action now.

DAY 8

What are You Thinking?

One of the most detrimental things that you can have is low/negative thinking. God said in II Corinthians 10:4, 5 (NIV), "The weapons we fight with are not the weapons of the world. On the contrary, they have divine power to demolish strongholds. We demolish arguments and every pretension that sets itself up against the knowledge of God, and we take captive every thought to make it obedient to Christ." Basically put, if you are not thinking like Christ, stop thinking. A lot of people fail to be financially prosperous because they fail to *think* they are. Sometimes, they think they don't deserve it, but why not? God said that we are the apples of His eye and we are joint heirs with Christ. Why should we have low thinking when our Heavenly Father created the universe?

Action steps:

Watch your thought-life carefully.

DAY 9

Power of the Tongue

Another thing that keeps people impoverished is the tongue. The tongue gets more people in trouble than almost anything else. People often do not recognize the power of the tongue. When you speak either positively or negatively, you set certain actions in motion. According to Proverbs 18:21 (NIV), "The tongue has the power of life and death, and those who love it will eat its fruit." The fact is, since we are created in God's image, we have the ability to create something out of nothing. All throughout Genesis 1, God spoke this world into existence. We have the same power. If you are broke, start saying that you are a multi-billionaire. Confess positivity over your life all day. Begin meditating on God's word and start saying what He says about your situation.

Action steps:

Make positive daily confessions aloud.

DAY 10

Fruit of the Spirit

Galatians 5:22, 23

But the fruit of the Spirit is love, joy, peace, patience, kindness, goodness, faithfulness, gentleness, and self-control. Against such things there is no law. Those who belong to Christ Jesus have crucified the sinful nature with its passions and desires. Since we live by the Spirit, let us keep in step with the Spirit. Let us not become conceited, provoking and envying each other.

I hope that you noticed that the scripture states "fruit" of the Spirit and not "fruits." So, if we walk in the fruit of the Spirit, we are operating the way God wants us to. If you have love, then you have joy and you have peace and you have patience and you have kindness and you are faithful and you are gentle and you have self-control.

Below is a brief checklist to see if you are operating in the fruit of the Spirit

Are you faithful or, do you fail to keep your word?

Can you control your spending habits?

Can you control your tongue?

Are you kind or rude?

Do you bring peace or are you a drama queen?

Are you harsh or are you gentle when you respond to people who get on your nerves?

Are you jealous of other people?

Remember that you can make your way prosperous by operating in the fruit of the Spirit.

Ask yourself:

Am I walking in the fruit of the Spirit or am I walking in the flesh?

DAY 11

Joshua and Caleb

Joshua and Caleb did not follow the crowd. When they were sent to spy on the Promised Land, their perspectives were totally different from that of the majority. When others doubted, they believed they were more than able to conquer and possess the land.

How do you feel about your situation? Do you have a tenacious spirit or a conquered spirit? The sad part is that not much has changed today. Most people want to follow the crowd and be "normal." In the U.S., debt is normal. But Dave Ramsey, the famous radio host and financial advisor, gives some good advice: "Debt is normal. Be Weird." God said owe no man anything except for the outstanding debt of love.

Action step:

Decide that you are more than able to conquer debt.

DAY 12

Forgiveness

Forgiveness is necessary for you to be prosperous in every area of your life – not just in your finances. Hebrews 12:15 (KJV) states, "lest any root of bitterness springing up trouble you, and thereby many be defiled." This means that unforgiveness causes bitterness. Holding grudges affects everyone around you.

Have you ever been around a person who has gone through an ugly divorce? If that person has not forgiven the ex, he or she can gain a negative outlook on the institution of marriage. That negative outlook can be passed along to the children. Now, the child has either a negative image regarding marriage or the child has to fight through the negative opinion of his/her parent.

The number one positive result of forgiveness is that it frees you up. The enemy wants to keep you bound up, make you trust no one, and keep you miserable.

Remember:

Jesus said, "Father forgive them for they know not what they do."
Jesus was an innocent man.

DAY 13

Who are You?

Another reason that people are not prosperous is that they do not know who they are. They run around spending loads of money so that they can look the part. They think that if they're wearing a $500 Armani suit, they are important or that people will like them. They do not realize that they have always been important. Ephesians 2:6 tells us: "And God raised us up with Christ and seated us with him in the heavenly realms in Christ Jesus." You can't get any higher than that. In Deuteronomy 32, God said that we are the apple of his eye. In Jeremiah 1, He said that before He formed us in our mothers' wombs, He knew us. People have to realize that God loves them. We serve a loving Father. So, the next time someone asks who you are, tell them that you are the child of the most high God!

Action Step:

Stop letting people validate you.

DAY 14

Focus

My favorite disciple is Peter. Peter was bold and courageous. It appeared that he was ready to fight at any given moment. The thing I like best about Peter is that he verified that it was Jesus bidding him to come and walk on the water.

Many times people say they hear God and they prematurely walk out on the water and have to suffer for it. Sometimes they act like Peter. They begin walking on the water. They do fine while their focus is on the Lord, but once their focus is off of the Lord, they begin to sink and to focus on the circumstances around them.

What makes you nervous, uneasy, and sleepless? Are you focused on what God says about your situation or do you listen to the media and make that your Gospel? Remember that God said He has overcome the world. That means that God is over all of the systems (i.e., financial systems) of the earth.

Action:

Meditate and confess what God says.

DAY 15

Are You a Joseph?

Two of the top problems in America today are that people are living above their means and they do not save money. Today's generation cannot rely on Social Security as part of their retirement income. Plus, many Americans do not have health insurance or they have to contribute toward the cost of their health insurance.

In Genesis, Joseph was able to rise above all obstacles (e.g., his brothers selling him into slavery, Potiphar's wife lying on him, and being stuck in jail while others were set free). But no matter what situation that he was in, he was able to rise to the top. Joseph had God's favor and wisdom on his life. He was even appointed as prime minister to the nation where he was able to save enough grain to take care of a nation and his family during the famine.

Ask yourself:

Are you a Joseph?
Do you consistently rise to the top during adverse situations?

DAY 16

Don't Lie

In Acts 5, many Christians were selling their properties and bringing the total proceeds to the apostles' feet so that they could distribute it to the poor. For some reason, though, Ananias and Sapphira got caught up and wanted to have the appearance that they were part of the program. To make it worse, both of them agreed to lie and say that they were giving the total proceeds. However, God gave Peter the word of knowledge and God gave them a second chance to vindicate themselves. They, however, chose to lie to the Holy Spirit. As a result, they both dropped dead instantly. So, when you give, please give from your heart and with the right intentions.

Remember:

Man looks at the outer appearance, but God looks at the heart.

DAY 17

Presence of Enemies

The two good things about your enemies are that they always point out areas of needed improvement and they definitely push you closer to God. In I Samuel 1, Peninnah teased Hannah because she was barren. God had closed Hannah's womb, but Hannah was so disheartened that she cried out to the Lord to receive her miracle. Although this verse specifically speaks about barrenness of the womb, life can be barren in other facets as well. Take a checking account, for instance.

Have you cried out to the Lord regarding your situation? You, too, can receive your miracle. After the prophet had witnessed her crying out to God, he stated in verse 17, "Go in peace, and may the God of Israel grant you what you have asked of him." In due time, Hannah became pregnant. After she cried out to God, the prophet declared her deliverance, and God granted her request.

Ask yourself: How do I treat or revere the man/ woman of God in my life?

Finally, Hannah promised God that she would give her child back to Him. This was really a first fruit offering. Have you promised God that you will give his portion back to Him once he gives you your financial breakthrough? Did you forget about Him?

Remember:

*Your enemies have divine purpose
in your life.*

DAY 18

Are You Part of the Kingdom?

God is sovereign. There is no higher authority than him. God's kingdom rules and reigns. He is the Alpha and Omega. However, every kingdom has certain rules and principles by which to live. Every Kingdom has its own governing system. According to Myles Monroe's book *Discovering the Kingdom*, tithing is part of God's economic system. Men cannot understand this kingdom because they are not part of this system, and they don't know the Lord. God said if you love Him, obey His commandments.

According to Matthew 6:33, God said to "seek ye first the Kingdom of God and his righteousness and all these things shall be added unto thee." You have to ask yourself if you are part of the kingdom or do you just have life insurance? We are to be living sacrifices. We cannot live and do like everyone else. Many people are not submitted to the Lord, so they are hindered from obtaining their financial breakthrough. Their lack of submission is evident by their lifestyles. We are under a sovereign authority and we should want to love God by our actions. That is why we cannot shack up before marriage. Matthew 7:21 states "everyone who cries Lord, Lord, shall not enter. I did that in your name and I did this in your name. God said that I don't know you, depart from me."

Remember:
Make sure that you really know the Lord. Don't play church.

DAY 19

Belief Versus Unbelief

Hebrews 4 speaks about belief. You must believe that God is faithful. God does not move in the realm of unbelief. All throughout the gospels, you see where Jesus was able to conduct miracles among believing people. These days, people often pray for something and then speak unbelief about it. What they don't realize is that they have cancelled their prayers by speaking unbelief. Remember that Deuteronomy tells us, "The word is near you. It is in your mouth. Speak life and not death."

God created the entire world by speaking it into existence. Since we are created in his image, we have the same power. Your belief in your prayers and in what you speak is what moves things in the spiritual realm. In Matthew 13, God speaks of a harvest that is 100-fold, 60-fold or 30-fold. Did you notice that the harvest was in descending order and not ascending? I wonder if it goes from 100-fold to 60-fold to 30-fold because of doubt and unbelief?

Remember:

Meditate on God's word so that it will get into your heart.

DAY 20

Are You Wicked?

Psalm 37:21 states that the wicked borrow and do not repay. Do you realize that every time you sign on the dotted line stating that you are going to pay a given amount, you have entered into a contract? If you purposely do not pay because of mismanagement of funds, God calls you wicked. God expects us to be good stewards. We are His ambassadors and we represent Him. The body of Christ is supposed to operate with integrity. Now, if there is a situation in which you honestly cannot pay, please contact your debtor and make payment arrangements.

Action item:

Get current on all of your bills.
Take the first steps toward getting out of debt!

DAY 21

Lack of Knowledge

God said in Hosea 4:6 (NIV), "My people are destroyed from lack of knowledge." He did not say that knowledge is not available. This verse implies that people reject knowledge probably because of fear, pride, laziness, or stupidity. Many people just do what they have been taught and do not have the courage to step out of their comfort zones. Habits are often passed down generationally. Sometimes people may have knowledge but don't apply it. In this day and time, with Internet accessibility, one can research and learn about almost any topic of interest. Due to the lack of applied knowledge, many people are not walking under the open heaven and their destiny. This is why many are suffering.

Reminder:

*Education is not limited to
what you learn in a classroom
environment.*

DAY 22

Count the Cost

The Lord said in Luke 14:28 (NIV), "Suppose one of you wants to build a tower. Won't you first sit down and estimate the cost to see if you have enough money to complete it?" This is one of my favorite scriptures. Basically, God is asking if you have thought about what you are trying to do. Have you done the numbers? God expects us to count the cost for every decision – especially financial ones. Many people get greedy or overextended. Then, they put the Lord to a test and expect God to pay for stuff that has nothing to do with Him. Remember, God pays for what He orders. In Proverb 10:28 it states, "The blessing of the Lord makes one rich and he adds no sorrow with it." So, if you are in a financial situation because you had to have some THING, you have to ask yourself, "Was this God's decision or my decision?"

Remember:

There is nothing wrong with taking a calculated risk.

DAY 23

Timing

Ecclesiastes 3:1 says, "There is a time for everything, and a season for every activity under the heavens." In Genesis 8:22 God said, "As long as earth endures, seedtime and harvest, cold and heat, summer and winter, day and night will never cease." You have to know God's timing for everything. You may have a God idea, but the wrong timing. In Malachi 3:11, God states, "Neither shall your vines cast their fruit before their time in the field." That's certainly another benefit of tithing! New believers sometimes get impatient when they start their walk with Christ. Many times they are looking for immediate results. But, you have to remember that God is a generational God and everything happens in its season. This is when you have to be very careful. You have to speak life over your situation – no matter what it looks like.

Remember:

Nothing happens before God's time.

DAY 24

Faith Without Works

James 2:14 states that faith without works is dead. People are often out of balance. Some have faith and no works; others have works and no faith. God wants us to have both. Your actions have to reflect your faith. It takes faith and works to get out of debt. After you have sowed in faith, believe that God will bless the work of your hands. You have to physically work toward your goal. You have to be a go-getter and you have to participate in your debt-freeness.

Remember:

God will do His part. Will you?

DAY 25

Make Disciples?

In Matthew 28:19 God says, "Therefore, go and make disciples of all nations...." Disciples are disciplined learners. Are you disciplined enough to learn and implement God's word – including what He says about finances? Being a disciplined learner will help you become prosperous – especially if you implement what you have learned. You must take action.

It is amazing what happens when you start moving forward. God starts removing the burdens. It is similar to when He told the 10 lepers to go and show themselves to the priest. As they were going forward, they were healed. Another part of being disciplined is being able to prioritize. According to Matthew 6:33, God says, "Seek me first ... and all things will be added." This basically means we should do everything His way, and He will take care of the rest.

Action step:

*Make sure that you make it
a priority to begin a financial plan TODAY!*

Day 26

Be Prosperous

God clearly stated in 3 John 1:2 that He wishes us to be "prosperous as well as our soul being prosperous." This makes it crystal clear that we are not supposed to be poor. According to Myles Munroe in <u>Rediscovering the Kingdom,</u> the condition of the people in a kingdom is a direct reflection of the king. For instance, it was obvious that Solomon was a great king at one time. It is mentioned in 1 Kings that when Queen Sheba showed up to meet Solomon, even the servants were loaded!

Remember:

We are a chosen generation.

DAY 27

Leave an Inheritance

Proverbs 13:22 tells us, "A good man leaves an inheritance for their children's children." Wow! God only calls him good. I wonder what it takes to be excellent! Since we are mainly talking about finances, how does a man leave an inheritance for his children? Here's how:

➤ Stop living for today. Understand the time value of money. For instance, $30/month for the next 35 years @ 10% interest rate is = to $65,000.

➤ Do you really need a new car? A new car loses 70% of its value over the first four years. You must realize every time that you spend a dime, you affect three to four generations after you. It is not just about you.

➤ Have you completed your estate planning? Do you have a will, durable power of attorney, and health-care surrogate? Do these forms need to be updated?

➤ Are you saving for retirement? If you have a company match, make sure that you contribute at least enough to earn that much. Have you done an analysis to see if you are saving enough to live comfortably at retirement?

➤ Do you have an emergency fund equal to three to six months worth of your living expenses?

➤ Are you saving for your child's education?

Remember:

"Watch the pennies, and the dollars will take care of themselves." (Dr. Dennis Kimbro in What Makes the Great Great)

DAY 28

Attitude of Gratitude

When you have a thankful spirit, it is amazing how God will move on your behalf. Psalms 100:4 advises us to "enter into his gates with thanksgiving." Why is it important to have a thankful spirit? It helps you to get into the Lord's presence. Getting into the Lord's presence and obtaining peace of mind is more important than anything. There are many financially wealthy people who do not have peace. Also, God said in Colossians that we should do all things without complaining.

Sometimes you don't miss something until you lose it. Maybe you lost a job or spouse because you were complaining all of the time. Remember that your words are powerful. You have the God-given ability to speak what you want into existence once you are in line with God's word.

Remember:

Be grateful.

DAY 29

The Blame Game

How many times are you going to blame other people for your circumstances? People will say, "Well, I did not finish school because my parents did not have the money" or "My husband left me with all of these kids." Well, that was 30 years ago! What about your money and your goals? Have you really exhausted all of your resources? What hidden talents do you have that have not been cultivated?

Sometimes dramatic situations do happen, but you cannot let them paralyze you and control your life. This is what happened at the healing pool in John 5. The man had been lying there for 38 years!! Stuck! I don't know what caused him to be stuck so long. I wonder what type of friends he had? Surely, within 38 years someone had to come with some recommendation for fixing his problem. I wonder if he was paralyzed by fear. The funny thing is that when Jesus asked him if he wanted to be healed, he gave Jesus the same old lousy excuse that he had been using for 38 years: "I have no one to help me."

Can you imagine Jesus asking you something and you responding like this man? Jesus never asked him if he needed help. He asked him if he needed *healing*. The man was probably assuming that the only way to get healed was by being in the pool when the angel stirred up the water. The man did not recognize that he was talking to the ultimate physician.

Action step:

Stop blaming others for where you are.

DAY 30

God, the Business Man

Did you know that God is an investment banker? Did you know that God is looking for a return on his investment? According to Matthew 25:15, God gives you talents (i.e., money) according to your ability. In this passage, God gave one man five talents, another man two, and another man one. Why did he do that? He did it because, respectively, that was all they could handle. Likewise, God may give some of you $10,000, $5,000, or $1,000 per month according to what you can handle. You may ask God why he only gave you a particular amount of money. Then He will ask you, "What did you do with what I gave you?"

In Matthew 25:19, he returned and settled the accounts. The ones to whom he gave five and two talents had doubled their portions. The one to whom he gave one talent had hidden his. If God asked you to give an account of the finances he gave you, will you have doubled what he gave you or are you in the negative? Are you making a profit? If not, what changes do you need to make to make a profit? Please be mindful that God is not going to continue throwing resources your way for you to mismanage them.

This is why the rich get richer and the poor get poorer. The rich typically invest in appreciating assets (e.g., stocks and bonds). The poor typically invest in depreciating assets (e.g., clothes, cars, cell phones).

Reminder:

Don't be like the one who received one talent.
Make sure that you properly invest what
God has given you.

DAY 31

Honor...

Exodus 20: 12, NIV, states, "Honor your father and mother, so that you may live long in the land the Lord your God is giving you."

You may say, "What does honoring my father and mother have to do with my finances?" It has everything to do with your finances because it is a Kingdom of God principle. If you follow God's principles you will prosper financially, emotionally, and physically. This is the first commandment that God attached a condition to. Basically, if you honor your parents, you will live long. If you don't honor your parents, you won't live long. God did not put a conditional disclaimer in the Bible to get around this. Even, if you had horrible parents, you are to honor the position that they hold in your lives. This is non-negotiable.

Action Item:

Honor your parents so that you will have a long, healthy, and financially prosperous life.

DAY 32

Husbands:
Live with Your Wives

Hey, fellas! I've got another golden nugget for you. God said in 1 Peter 3:7, "…live with your wives, and treat them with respect as the weaker partner and as heirs with you as the gracious gift of life, so that nothing will hinder your prayers." Wow…this is amazing to me. God basically said, if you don't live with your wife and respect her, He really is not hearing you. There is static between God and you if you mistreat your wife.

Obviously, this impacts your household income. You may have many reasons why you think you have the right to mistreat your wife. However, through the lens of God, you don't.

Now, if you have children, your children are watching how you treat your wife. You really have to be careful, because you don't want to inject a generation curse; you want to inject a generational blessing.

Remember, you are the head of the household, and God holds you accountable for everything.

Action Steps:

Treat your wife right and everything else will follow, including the money.

DAY 33

Ladies:

Respect Your Husbands!

Isn't it strange that God said to respect your husbands. In Ephesians, 5:33, NIV, it states, "...a wife must respect her husband." I was really shocked. I thought God would say "wife you must love your husband." Wow, I wonder why he said that.

Let's dig deeper.

The definition of respect, according to Webster, is:

1. A relation or reference to a particular thing or situation

2. An act of giving particular attention: Consideration

3. High or special regard: Esteem

Wow, there you go. We are to be considerate and we are to hold our husbands in high esteem. That does not mean that we are to agree with them all of the time. But, we are to be cognizant of the place we chose for them to have in our lives.

Why is respect important to a marriage? Respecting your husband can help save your marriage and help keep families together. Keeping families together is a vital key in achieving financial prosperity.

Action Item:

Let's respect our husbands!

DAY 34

Stay Together

If you are married, God wants you to stay together. Now, there are reasons in the Bible for divorce; however, the original intent of God was for couples to stay together. In Malachi, 2:16, NIV: "I hate divorce," says the LORD God of Israel.

Why does God hate divorce?

1. Marriage relationship is a covenant, not a contract. It should only be broken by death. The marriage relationship is a reflection of Jesus and the Bride of Christ, which is the church.

2. One of the purposes of the marriage is to have Godly offspring, as per Malachi 2:15. This is one way that God builds His Kingdom on earth because the parents are to teach the children the ways of the Lord.

3. When one goes through a divorce, one will suffer financially, emotionally, and spiritually. It makes it more difficult to pass on an inheritance.

Now, if you have gone through a divorce, God still loves you, and the blood of Jesus covers every situation.

Action Step:

Invite God into your marriage.
Don't leave Him at the wedding altar.

DAY 35

Work Ethics

One way to prosper financially is to make sure you have excellent work ethics. Colossians 3:23-24 states, "Whatever you do, work at it with all your heart, as working for the Lord, not for human masters, since you know that you will receive an inheritance from the Lord as a reward. It is the Lord God you are serving."

In today's society, it is hard trying to find people who have decent work ethics. Some people want to have every Friday off, or if they are at working they are surfing the Internet or talking about nothing all day. This is not honoring the Lord.

As Christians, we are to be the best employees we can be. Our bosses should not have to worry about us slacking off or doing a shabby job.

Also, we are to work unto the Lord even if we have a difficult boss. Sometimes the difficult boss has no idea who the real boss is, and we may be the only light in darkness that he sees.

Remember:

Be the best. God is watching.

DAY 36

Promotion Comes from God, Not Man!

As we continue to work for the Lord in our respective fields, remember that promotion comes from the Lord, not man. Psalm 75:6, 7 states, "No one from the east or the west or from the desert can exalt themselves. It is God who judges: He brings one down, he exalts another."

This scripture is dear to my heart. I was working somewhere for 12 years. For some reason, my manager and her manager did not like me even though I was faithful and productive. Their goal was to get rid of me. Every day they would walk through the aisle just to make sure that I was at work on time, or they would monitor how long I was in the bath room. It was really a crazy time in my life. They even pulled my credit for six consecutive months trying to find something.

However, I was familiar with this scripture. Out of the blue, a former boss from 11 years prior called and offered me a job at another company with more pay and a better work atmosphere.

Remember:

God is faithful and he will reward you!

Day 37

Praise

Did you know that praise is a weapon? II Corinthians 10:4 states, "The weapons we fight with are not the weapons of the world. On the contrary, they have divine power to demolish strongholds."

Now, you may ask what is a stronghold? In this scripture, a stronghold is a demonic fortress of thoughts housing evil spirits that:

1. Control, dictate, and influence your attitudes and behavior
2. Oppress and discourage you
3. Filter and color how you view or react to situations, circumstances, or people.

One weapon that you have in your arsenal is to praise God without ceasing. You have to open your mouth, clap your hands, dance, or do something to praise God. Praising God changes the atmosphere. When you praise God, you are getting God's attention. The bible says that God inhabits in the praises of His people. So when you praise God, you are clearing the way to be ushered in the presence of the Lord and His heavenly Host!

By praising God, this will help pull down the strongholds that influence your thinking pattern. You have to praise Him to hear His voice so that He can lead you to a wealthy place.

Action:

Praise Him NOW!

DAY 38

Jealous God

Did you know that God is a jealous God? In Exodus 20: 3-6, states, "You shall have no other gods before me. You shall not make for yourself an image in the form of anything in heaven above or on the earth beneath or in the waters below. You shall not bow down to them or worship them; for I, the Lord your God, am a jealous God, punishing the children for the sin of the parents to the third and fourth generation of those who hate me, but showing love to a thousand generations of those who love me and keep my commandments."

Did you ever think that one of the reasons you are struggling financially is that you have your priorities backwards and God is trying to get your attention? We may or may not have physical idols that we create, but there other idols that take our attention from God. For instance, you may spend too much time watching television and not studying His word, which teaches you how to make your way prosperous.

Sometimes God has to shake things up to get your focus back on Him.

Action Step:

Always place God first.

DAY 39

Blessings and Curses

Deuteronomy 28 is a power-pack chapter of the Bible that basically lists all of the benefits of obeying God and all of the curses that shall come upon you if you disobey God.

In summary, God is saying you will be blessed in the country and in the city. Your job will be blessed. Your purpose in life will not be aborted. Everything you do will be blessed.

If you choose not to follow God's pattern, you will be cursed. Your bloodline will be cursed for three to four generations. You will have confusion of mind. The woman you want to marry will be given to another.

Action step:

Obey God!

DAY 40

Stand

Ephesians 6:10-20 is one of my favorite scriptures. I especially like Ephesians 6: 13b: "...and after you have done everything to stand." What does it mean to stand?

First, let us define the word stand. In this context, it is used as an infinitive verb. Webster defines the word stand as follows:

1. To endure or undergo successfully
2. To tolerate without flinching: bear courageously
3. To endure the presence or personality of

Obviously, this scripture was written for those who are undergoing a test. God wants us to endure until the end. He wants us to endure in a manner that represents Him and He wants us to be courageous in our posture. Never forget that we are light in darkness and others observe how we go through the fire. Finally, when the enemy is in your face, you have the authority to bind the demonic forces that are moving against you and to speak God's word over the situation.

God has instructed us to keep standing the test of time as true soldiers. After you have been obedient to God's word, after you have been a good steward over your finances, after you have continually made your confessions, and after you have been faithful to your employer, keep standing.

Remember:

God also said "you shall reap a harvest if you faint not!" Don't Faint!